GROW YOUR OWN MONEY !!

By Richard A Burritt

New Buy and Sell Indicators

Fully Disclosed

Best for 401k's, IRA's and Mutual Funds

Contents

What do I mean when I say "Grow Your Own Money"? Unless you know a financial advisor who you can show you a documented track record of buying near the bottom and selling near the top, you can do better on your own by following the plan specified in this book.

The question I have for all of you is this. Are you satisfied with the returns of your 401 k, your IRA, or your mutual funds? Given the horrific recession from which we are beginning to emerge, my guess is that the vast majority of you are not at all satisfied. In fact, there have been reports that many people are not even looking at their statements or, at best, giving them a cursory glance in order not to feel the pain of their retirement funds shrinking away. This has to change. There has to be a better way to avoid most of the pain when a major recession rears its ugly head. Good news, there is a better way than the old buy and hold method. There is also a better way than the in and out trading based on greed and fear.

Throughout the course of this book I will attempt to show you how, using about fifteen minutes a month of your time, you can get out of the market near the top and get back in near the bottom. Please notice I said NEAR the top and NEAR the bottom. Those of you who are looking to sell out AT the top and buy back in AT the bottom are looking for the holy grail which is unattainable to us mortals.

Let's look at a hypothetical example called buy and hold Bridget. A little over ten years ago, Bridget changed jobs and rolled her 401k into a self-directed IRA. She had $10,000 to invest and after checking around and asking all the right questions she settled on a very highly rated conservative mutual fund called American Funds Mutual A. On December 27th, 1999 she purchased 424 shares. She elected to take her distributions in cash and on November 30th, 2009 her 424 shares were worth $9693. Not a happy camper.

You may recall the dot-com bubble and may also remember those day-traders who were making tons of money. Where are they now? The vast majority gave it all back and more. Since investing is a zero-sum game, where has all the money gone? Eventually, most of it goes to Wall St. where exorbitant salaries and huge bonuses are the norm. The average investor has little chance against the pros with their supercomputers and brilliant algorithms.

If you don't have a good plan, you need one! You will be reading about a good plan right here, in this book. There is a caveat. There will be times when this plan may appear to be not working. During these times, patience is a virtue. This plan is based on the one thing that really keeps our country great. For now, I'm going to call it the Mystery Number. It will be fully revealed to you later in this book along with the philosophy behind it.

I'm sure some, or many of you would like to know what to invest in. I personally like mid-cap growth funds. If you have a 401k at work, there should be a mid-cap choice. If you have a self-directed IRA, my top choice is the S&P Mid-cap fund which is traded every business day just like a stock. The symbol is MDY.

The choice of broker is up to you. I use a discount broker as I don't want anyone disrupting my thoughts so they can sell me something. It is easy to compare MDY to any other mutual fund or index. Just go to Big Charts.com on your computer. It's free which is always good. Type in MDY and hit interactive charting. It may take a little while to come up. On the left side enter the mutual fund symbol. Right above where it says index. I put in AMARX, which is the symbol for American Funds Mutual A. Hit one decade and see the difference.

There is a major point that can't be expressed strongly enough. This plan is only for long term investors who invest in equities by using mutual funds, 401k's and IRA's. If your outlook shifts from long term to short term you will, in all likelihood, lose money. If you switch to individual stocks or industries you may also lose. As mentioned before, there will be times when this plan may appear to be not working. These are times when the market is influenced by factors not specifically related to the overall well-being of our economy. As you look at each individual chart from 1980 thru 2009 an attempt to briefly explain what happened and why will accompany each chart.

2009
Mystery # vs Dow

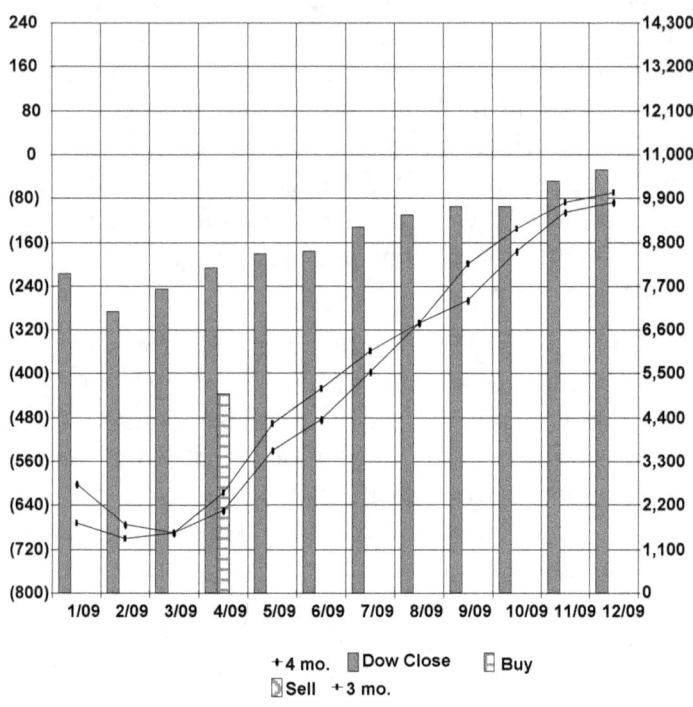

Here is the explanation of the chart you saw on the last page. The dark vertical bars show the closing price of the Dow Jones Industrial Average as measured by the numbers on the right. The lighter gray single vertical bar at 4/2009 is the buy signal, the height of which is of no consequence except to differentiate from a sell signal which will be significantly taller. The solid black line is a four month moving average of the mystery number which generates sell signals. The dotted black line is a three month moving average of the mystery number which generates buy signals. Both the solid black line and the dotted black line are depicted on the chart to match the vertical set of numbers on the left side of the chart.

A buy signal is given when the dotted black line moves higher for two consecutive months. A sell signal is given when the solid black line moves lower for two consecutive months AND moves below the zero line on the chart. These last two sentences constitute the only rules for generating buy and sell signals.

Some of you may be thinking, OK, how do I get those three months and four month moving averages? It's really not hard. All you need to do to generate a four month moving average is; 1. Record the mystery number when it comes out for four consecutive months. 2. Add up the four numbers and divide by four and record that number. That number is recorded each month using the new mystery number and the three previous numbers. Remember you are looking for a sell signal when doing the four month moving average. The three month moving average is the same except you add up only the most recent three mystery numbers and divide by three.

When you have received a buy signal and acted upon it you are looking for a sell signal. When you have received a sell signal and acted upon it you are looking for a buy signal. The fact that you may have received consecutive buy or sell signals is of no consequence.

The previous chart has given us a clear buy signal in April of 2009. At this time it appears to be an excellent signal as the Dow closed at 7609 at the end of March and at 10,345 at the end of November.

The chart for 2008 will be put up on the next page. It will show the sell signal generated in April of 2008 when the Dow closed at the end of March at 12,263. To do the math, if you sold out at 12,263 and bought back in at 7609 and had a value of 10,345 at the end of November, you would have avoided a loss in Dow points,(which are not dollars), of 4654 and gained 2736. A very rewarding experience!

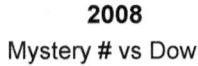

2008

Mystery # vs Dow

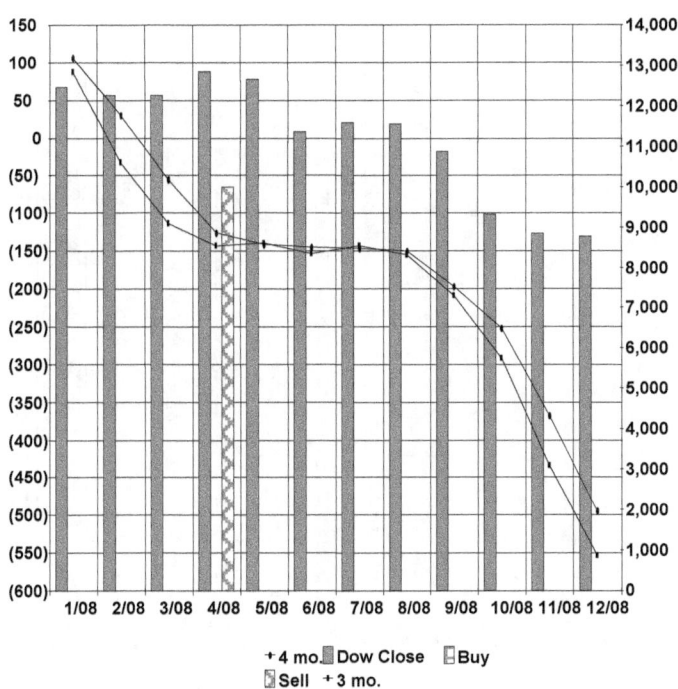

Notice how the four month moving average, depicted by the solid black line, moved lower for two months in a row AND moved below the zero line. This sell signal, if acted upon, would have prevented a big loss.

Next chart.

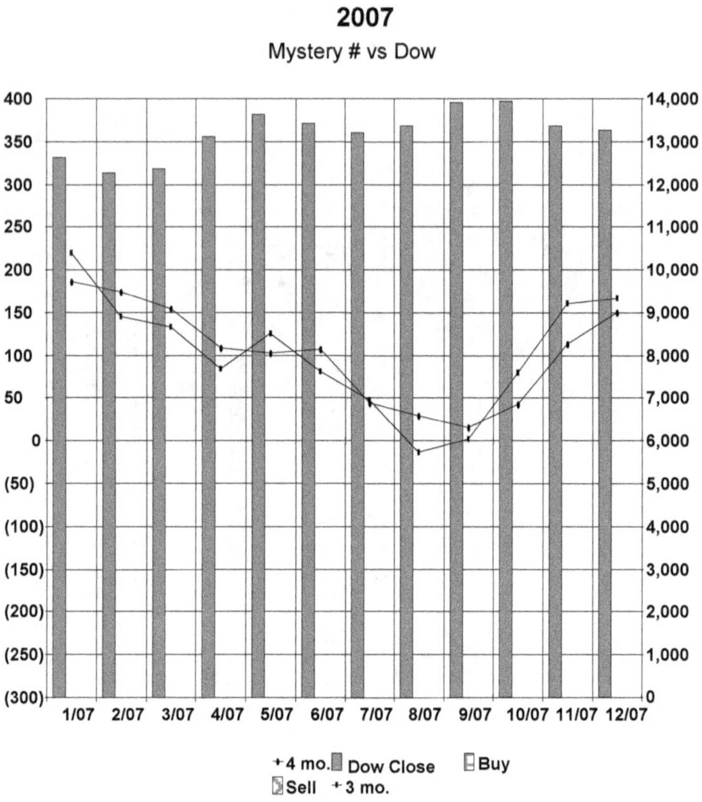

2007
Mystery # vs Dow

| | 400 | | | | | | | | | | | | 14,000 |

(chart: 2007 Mystery # vs Dow — bar chart with Dow Close bars and moving-average lines)

Left axis values: 400, 350, 300, 250, 200, 150, 100, 50, 0, (50), (100), (150), (200), (250), (300)

Right axis values: 14,000, 13,000, 12,000, 11,000, 10,000, 9,000, 8,000, 7,000, 6,000, 5,000, 4,000, 3,000, 2,000, 1,000, 0

X-axis: 1/07 2/07 3/07 4/07 5/07 6/07 7/07 8/07 9/07 10/07 11/07 12/07

Legend: + 4 mo. ■ Dow Close ▯ Buy ▨ Sell + 3 mo.

Notice how the Dow was moving higher for the first nine months of the year. At the same time the moving average lines were showing weakness. Nothing to buy or sell this year. Remember, the previous chart had one signal, which was a sell. So we are currently in the market, making money! Next chart.

2006
Mystery # vs Dow

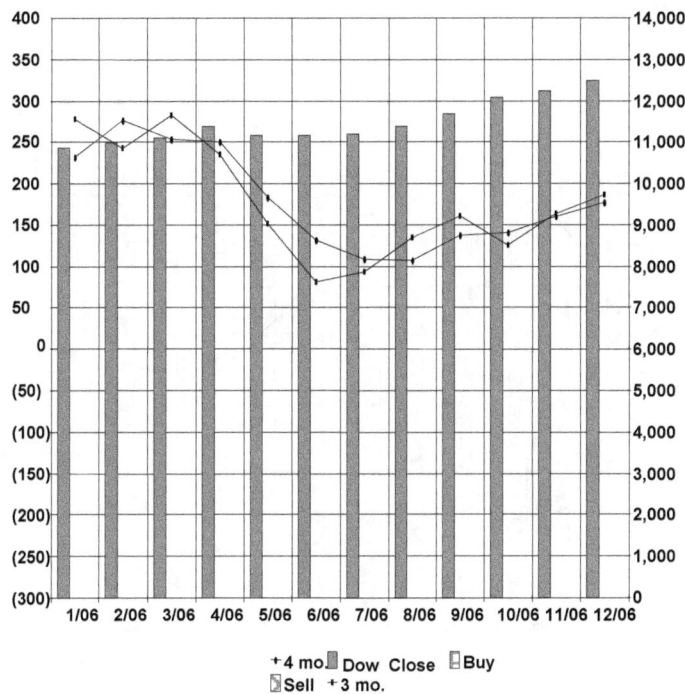

Nothing to do here. We are long the market (last signal was a buy). Happily making money!

Next chart.

2005
Mystery # vs Dow

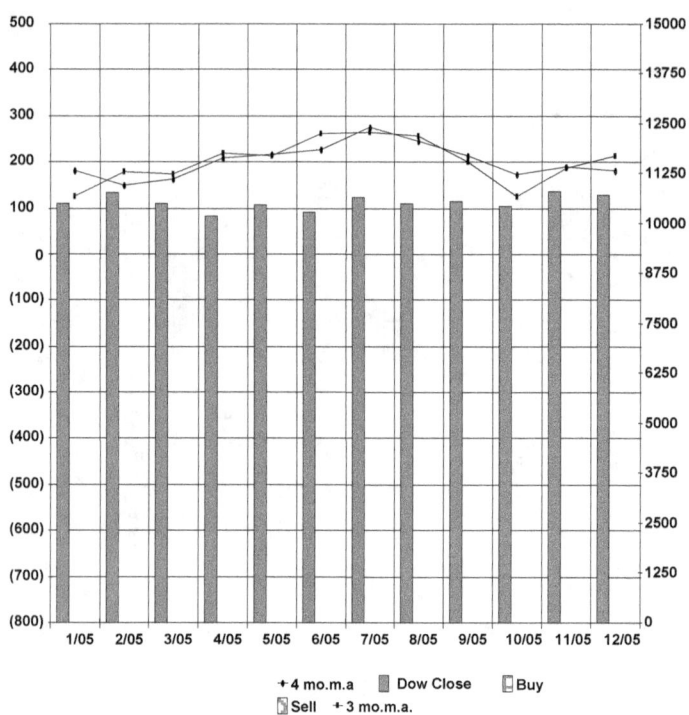

Same scenario. It's good to be boring sometimes. Next chart.

OK, so lets review. So far, since Jan. 2005 we have had only two signals, a sell signal from April 2008 and a buy signal from April 2009 which avoided a 56.95% loss in the Dow.

That was huge. The gain since the April 2009 buy signal has amounted to a 26.6% gain in the Dow - another very good number that justifies following this plan. Now for the next chart.

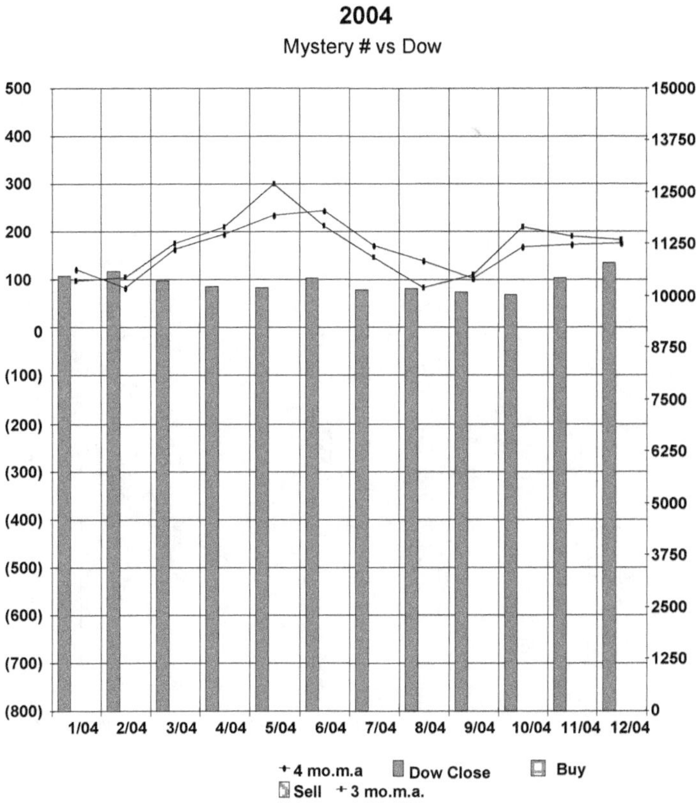

2004

Mystery # vs Dow

Once again, we are long the market, just where we want to be.

2003
Mystery # vs Dow

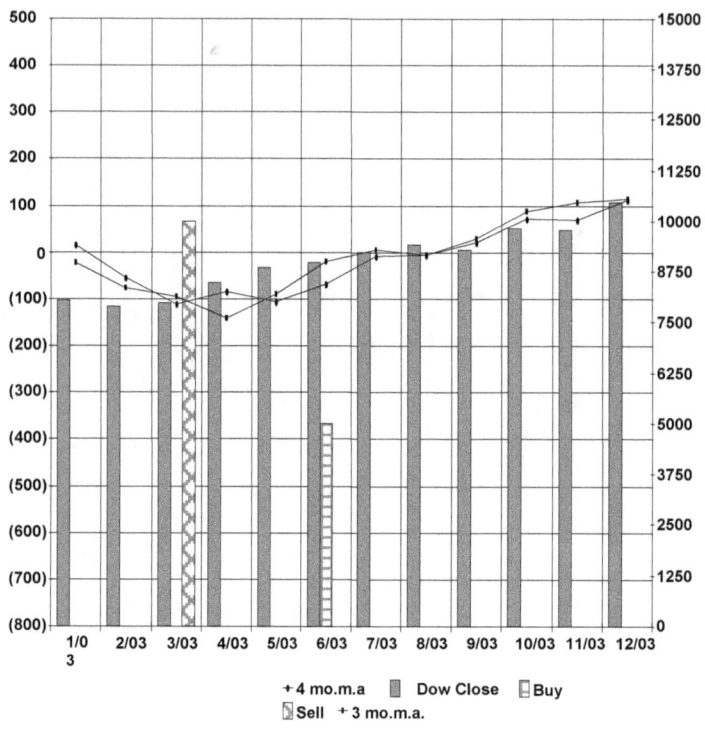

+4 mo.m.a   ■ Dow Close   ▨ Buy
▨ Sell   +3 mo.m.a.

Well here's some action, let's talk about it. The solid black four month moving average gave a sell signal in March of 2003 when it went down for two consecutive months AND went below the zero line. At this point the chances of a recession are high due to the mystery line prediction. Just three months later, the dotted black three month moving average gave us a buy signal. Possible recession averted. Took an 11% loss that was necessary to avoid the possibility of a much larger loss. You can't win them all but sometimes discretion is the better part of valor. Now for the positive buy signal that happened in June of 2003.

If you didn't become discouraged and say to yourself, this isn't working, I have to find a better way, you were highly rewarded. That buy signal lasted until April of 2008, which translated into a GAIN in Dow points of greater than 42%. Have a little faith. Next chart.

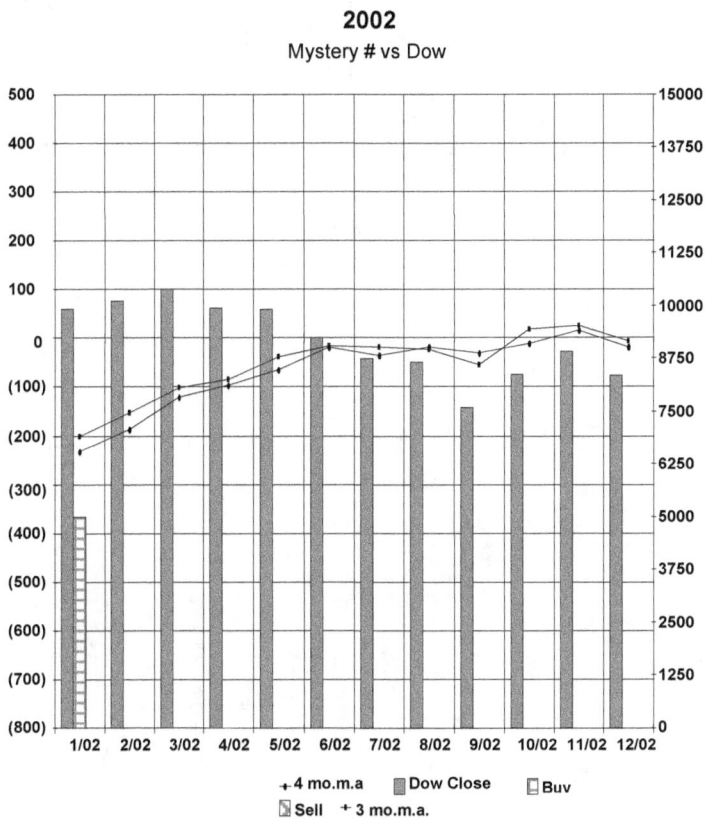

2002
Mystery # vs Dow

A buy signal in Jan. Coming out of the emotional trauma that gripped the nation after 9/11. From June on, the buy and sell lines are wavering between possible recession and possible expansion. Bought high in Jan.

2002 and sold low in March of 03. Got whipsawed. It happens when there is economic indecision. Lost 19.4% As a way of further explanation, the whole period from 2001 thru the middle of 2003 reflected a very emotional and indecisive time in our nations history. From the bursting of the dot-com speculative bubble to the 9/11 event to the fear of more potential terrorism to the grim reality of warfare, came economic uncertainty that led to the mystery number being whipped back and forth and preclude solid growth in our economy. The next chart will display the beginning of this period as the buy and sell lines drop below the zero line. Next chart.

2001

Mystery # vs Dow

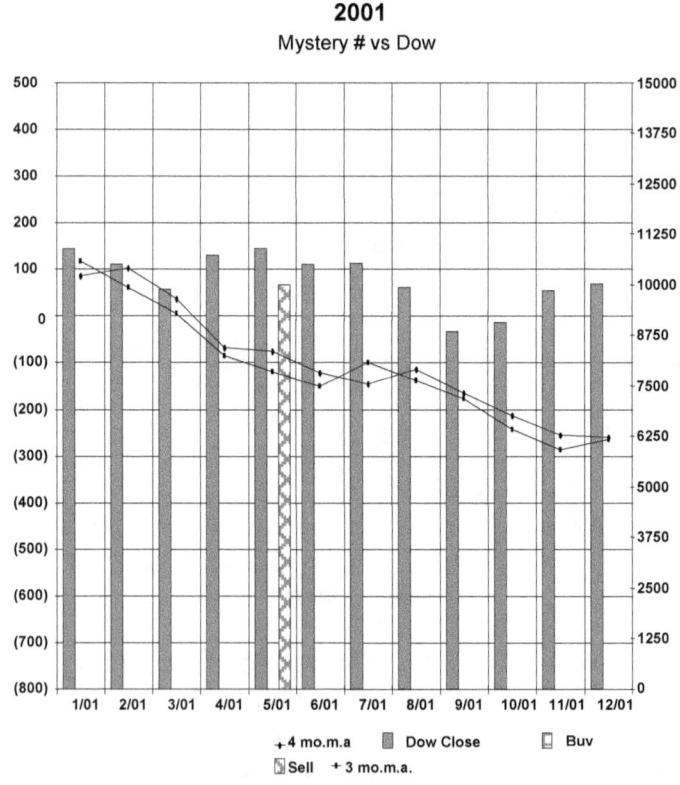

As mentioned, this is the beginning of economic uncertainty. Notice where the zero line is being penetrated to the downside. Next chart.

2000

Mystery # vs Dow

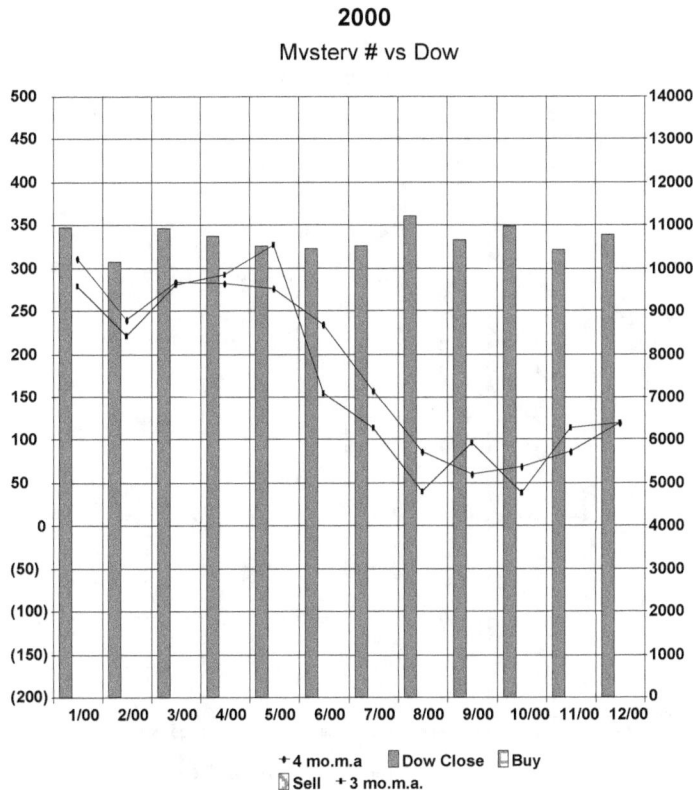

Notice how the buy/sell lines start to decline in June even while the vertical bars of the Dow remain fairly constant. At this point we are long the market, the sell point is shown on the chart of 2001at 10,912. The buy signal that got us long the market, came way back in December of 1990 at 2634, a gain of 314% !! Not too shabby. At this point , in the interest of brevity, I could skip back to the 1990 chart but will not do that so those of you that are so inclined can follow the progression to gain insight and confidence in this long-term plan.

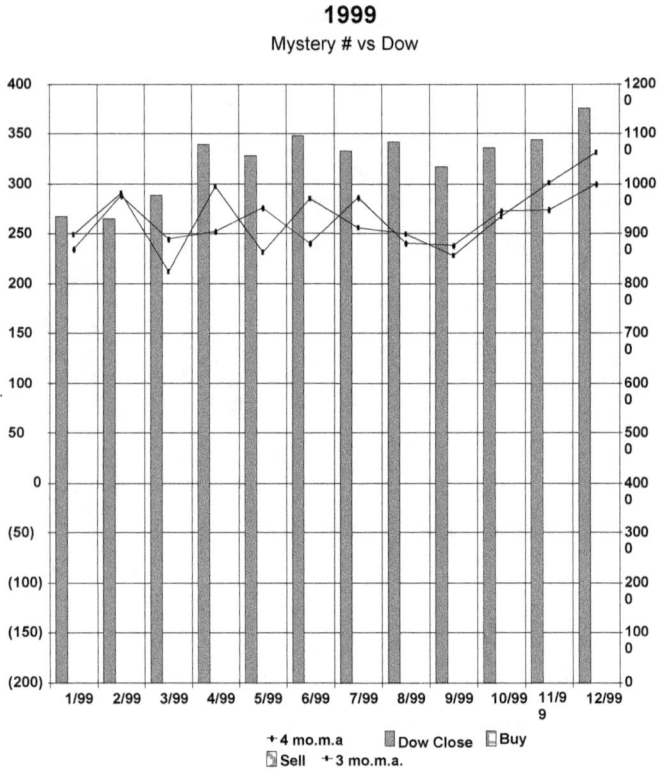

1999
Mystery # vs Dow

1998
Mystery # vs Dow

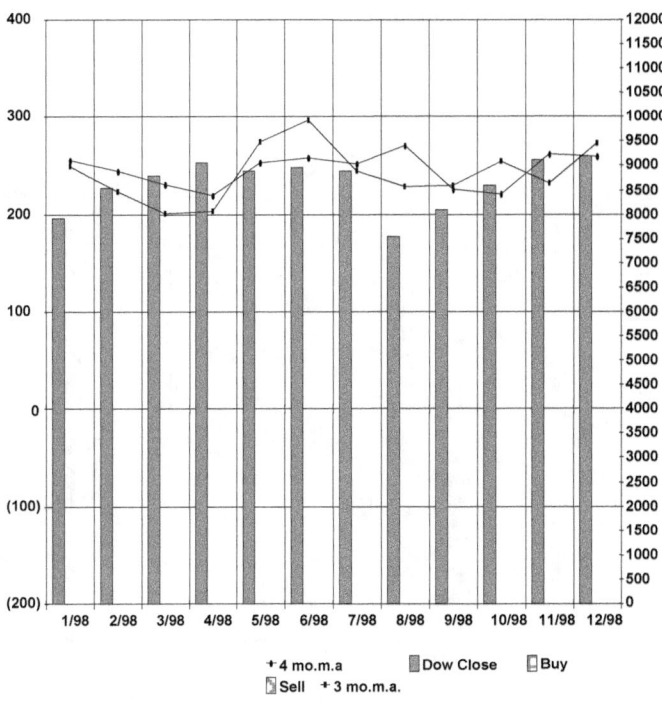

+ 4 mo.m.a   ▦ Dow Close   ▢ Buy

▨ Sell   + 3 mo.m.a.

1997
Mystery # vs Dow

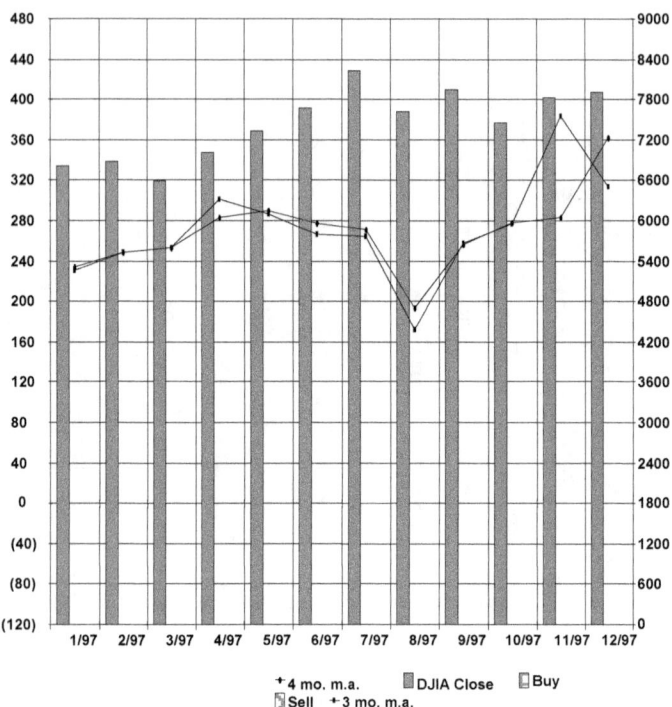

+ 4 mo. m.a.   ■ DJIA Close   ▫ Buy
▫ Sell   + 3 mo. m.a.

1996
Mystery # vs Dow

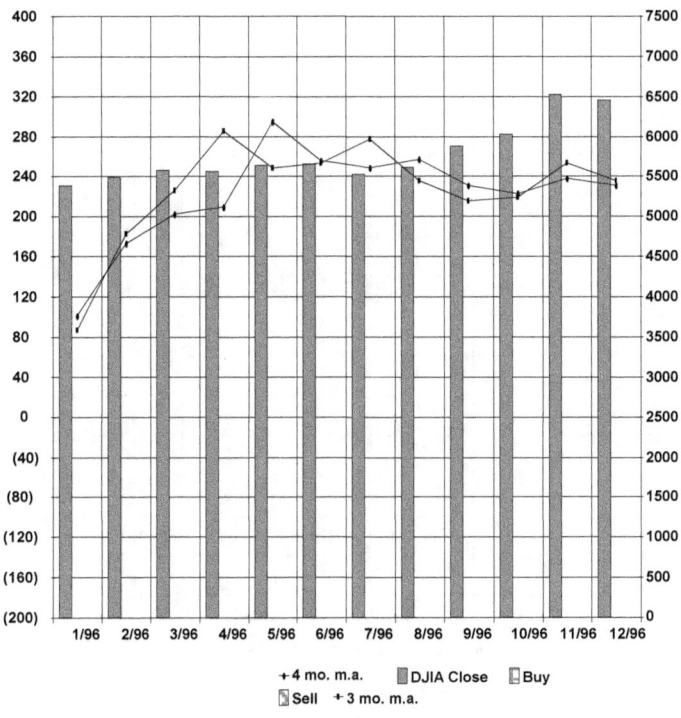

1995

Mystery # vs Dow

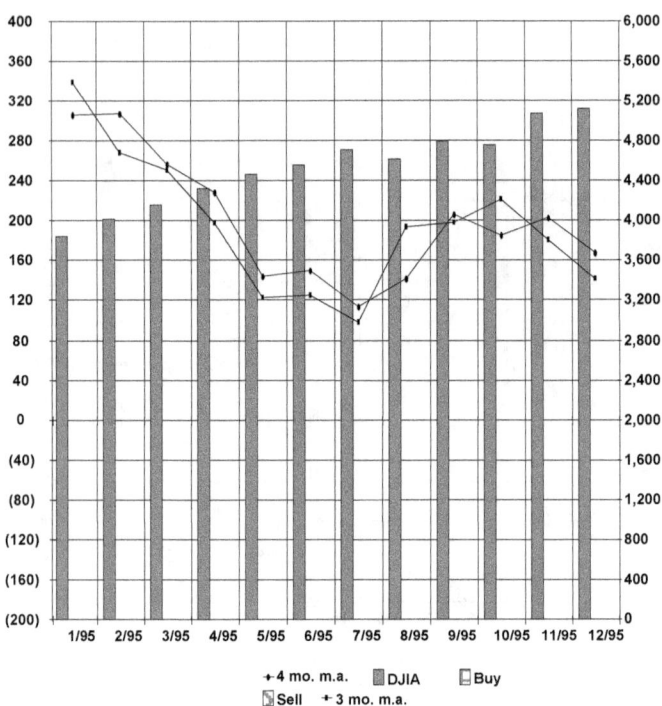

+ 4 mo. m.a.   ▓ DJIA   ▢ Buy
▨ Sell   + 3 mo. m.a.

1994
Mystery # vs Dow

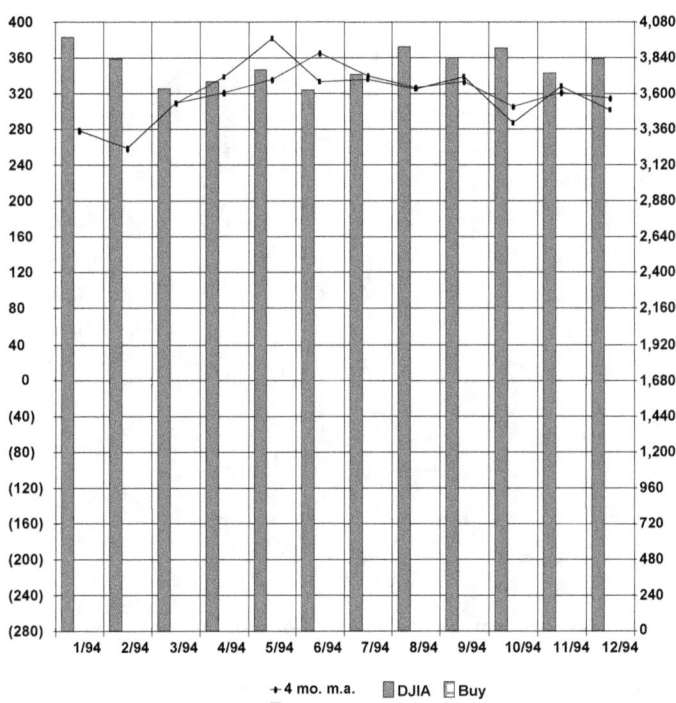

1993

Mystery # vs Dow

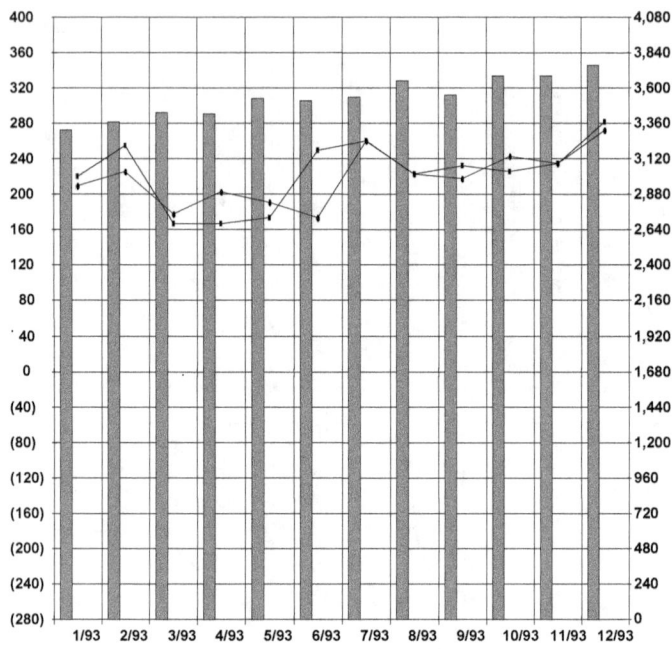

+ 4 mo. m.a. ■DJIA □Buy
▨Sell + 3 mo. m.a.

26

1992
Mystery # vs Dow

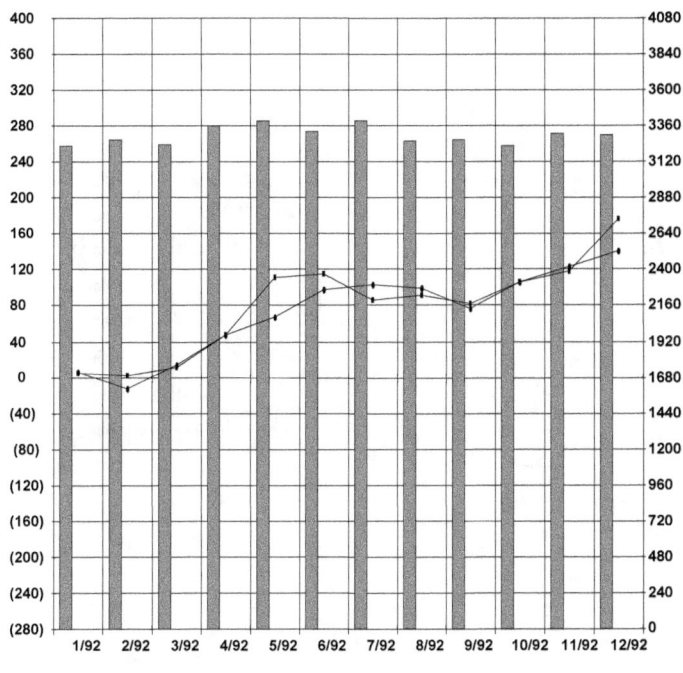

1991
Mystery # vs Dow

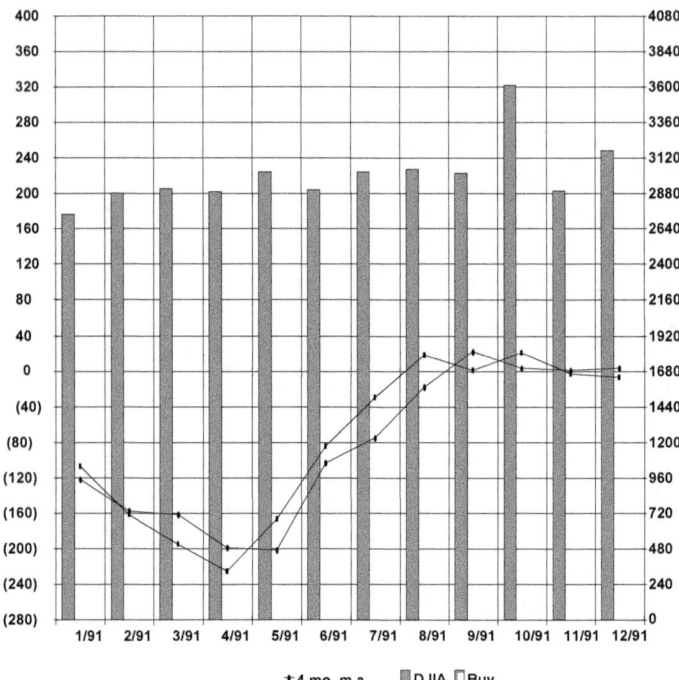

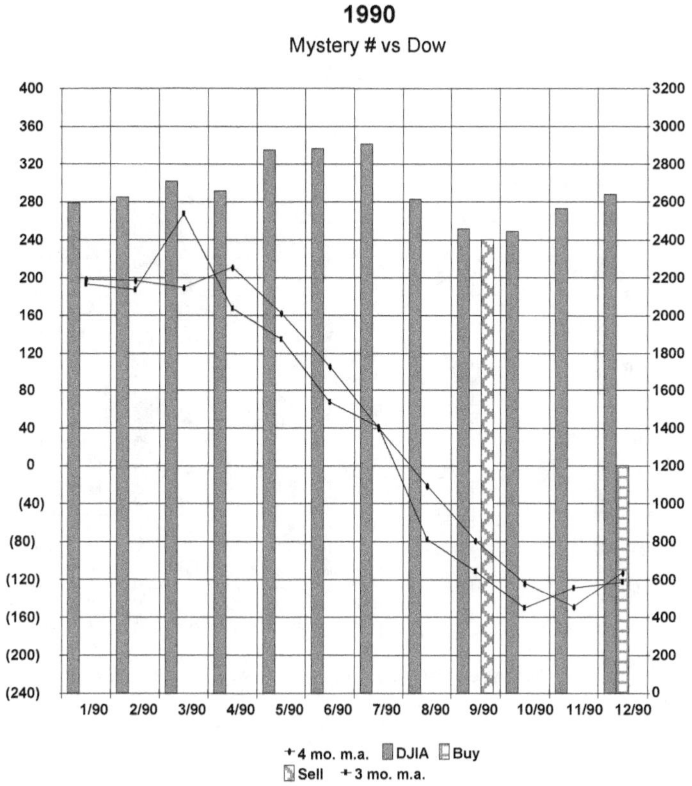

1990
Mystery # vs Dow

1/90	2/90	3/90	4/90	5/90	6/90	7/90	8/90	9/90	10/90	11/90	12/90

+ 4 mo. m.a. ▓DJIA ☐Buy
▨Sell + 3 mo. m.a.

Finally, some signals to discuss. Notice the solid black sell line went down for two consecutive months AND broke below the zero line, so a sell signal was generated with the Dow at 2452. At the end of Dec. the dotted black line went up for two consecutive months so we bought back in at 2634, a loss of over 7%. Remember the philosophy, we want to avoid the possibility of losing a lot of money in a deep recession. We did that and made a huge gain from our buy point at 2634.

1989

Mystery # vs Dow

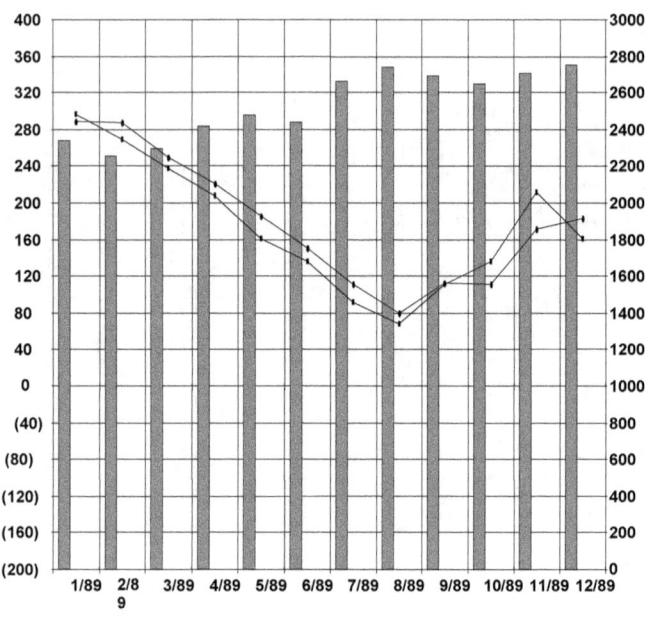

1988
Mystery # vs Dow

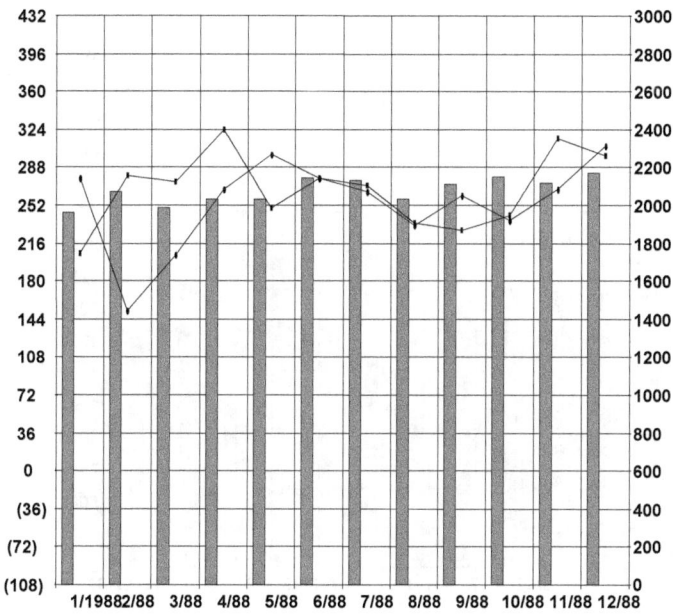

⁺4 mo. m.a. ▧DJIA▧Buy
▧Sell ⁺3 mo. m.a.

31

1987
Mystery # vs Dow

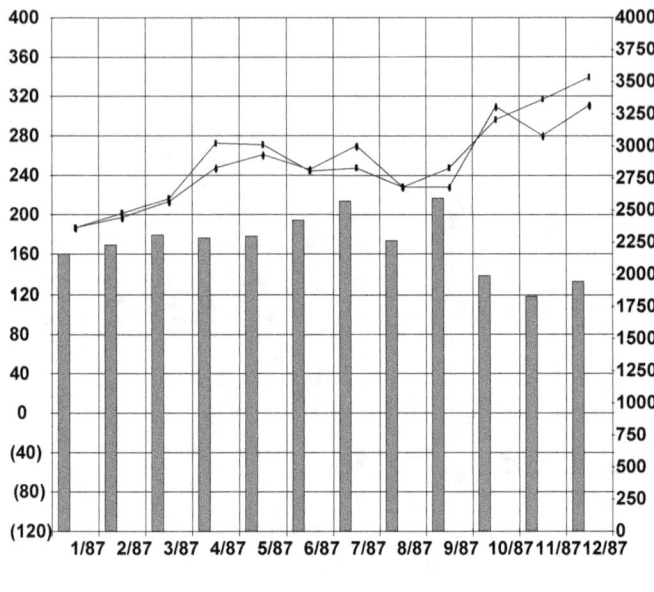

+ 4 mo. m.a.   ■ DJIA Close   ⊟ Buy
▨ Sell   + 3 mo. m.a.

    Notice how the buy/sell lines ignored the 500 point drop in the Dow in October, commonly called Black Monday. A buying opportunity for both long term investors and short term traders.

1986

Mystery # vs Dow

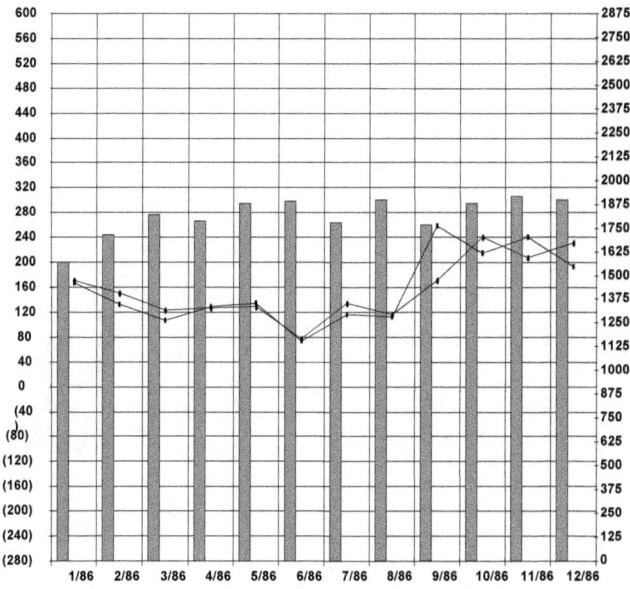

+ 4 mo. m.a.　　■ DJIA Close　□ Buy
□ Sell　+ 3 mo. m.a.

33

1985

Mystery # vs Dow

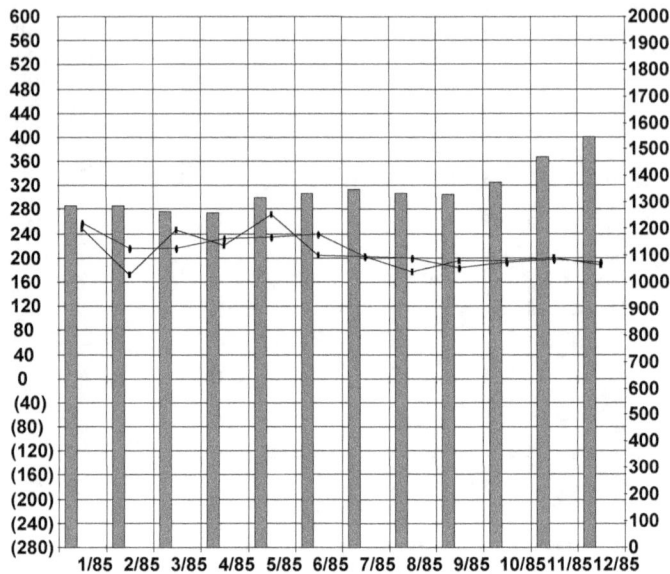

+ 4 mo. m.a. ▓DJIA Close   ⊟Buy
▨Sell + 3 mo. m.a.

1984
Mystery # vs Dow

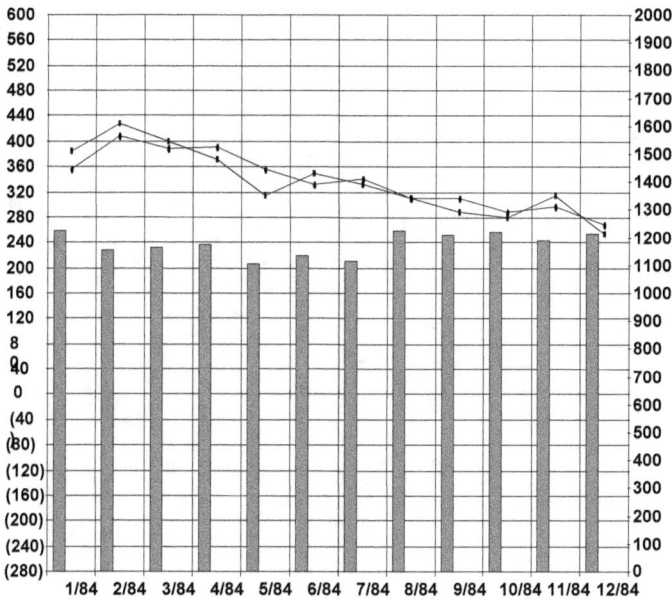

+4 mo. m.a.　■ DJIA Close　🗆 Buy
🔲 Sell　+3 mo. m.a.

35

1983
Mystery # vs Dow

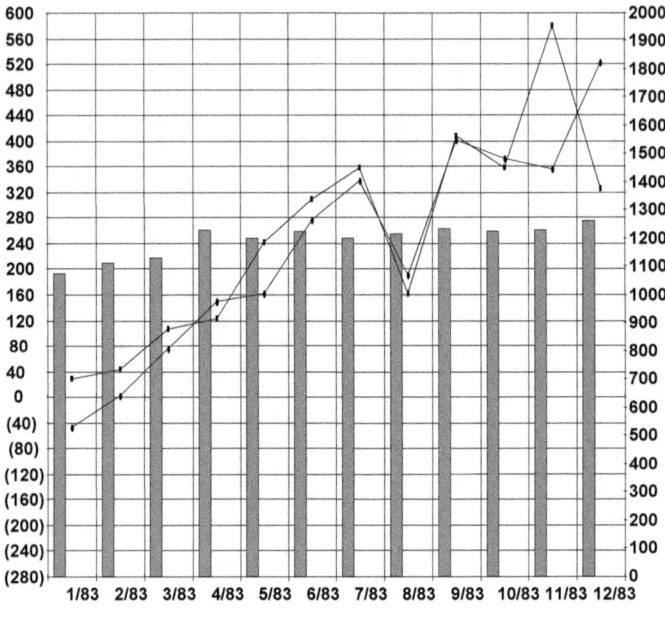

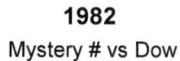

1982

Mystery # vs Dow

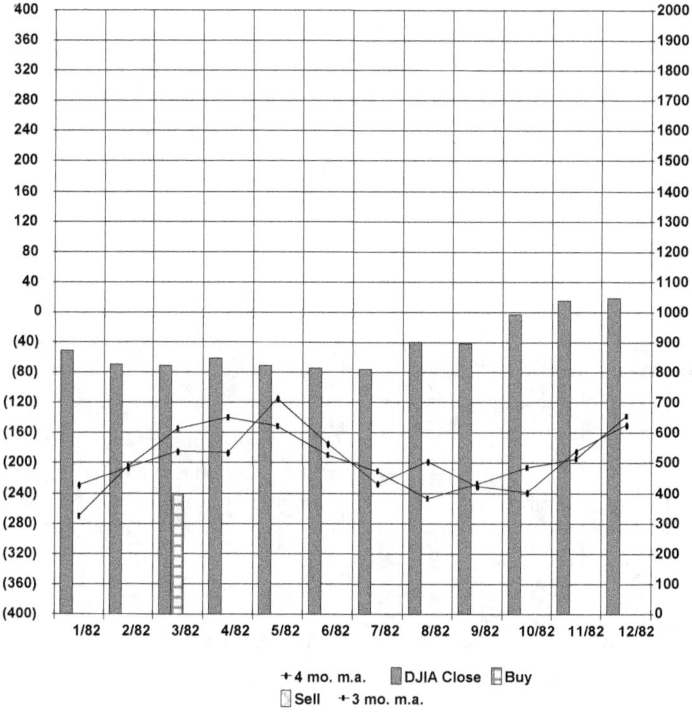

400	2000
360	1900
320	1800
280	1700
240	1600
200	1500
160	1400
120	1300
80	1200
40	1100
0	1000
(40)	900
(80)	800
(120)	700
(160)	600
(200)	500
(240)	400
(280)	300
(320)	200
(360)	100
(400)	0

1/82 2/82 3/82 4/82 5/82 6/82 7/82 8/82 9/82 10/82 11/82 12/82

+4 mo. m.a. ■DJIA Close ▯Buy
▯Sell +3 mo. m.a.

On this chart we have a buy signal for March at 823. Recall our sell signal came in Sept. 1990 at 2452. A very nice gain of nearly 198%.

1981

Mystery # vs Dow

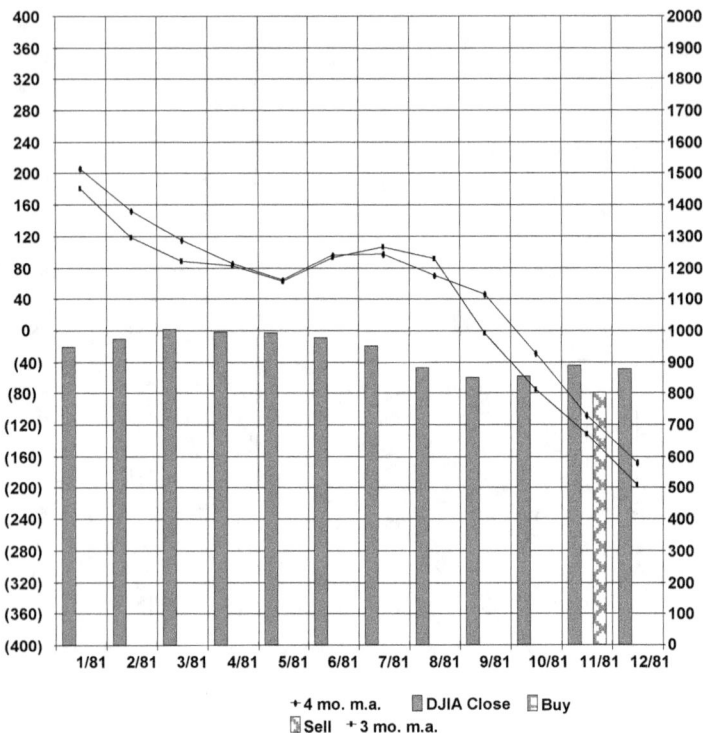

+ 4 mo. m.a.   ■ DJIA Close   ⊟ Buy
⬚ Sell   + 3 mo. m.a.

This chart shows a sell signal for Nov. at 889. Remember we had a buy signal for March of 1982 at 823. A gain of 8%.

1980

Mystery # vs Dow

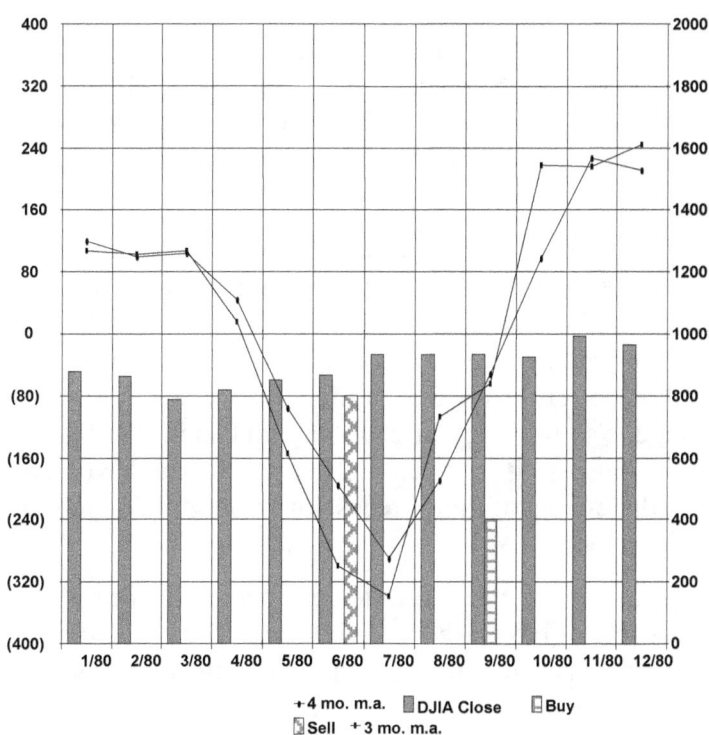

+4 mo. m.a. ▊DJIA Close ▤Buy
▥Sell +3 mo. m.a.

This chart shows a buy for Sept. at 932. We sold in Nov. 1981 at 889. A loss of 4.7%. We also show a sale for June at 868. A loss of 7%.

Let's summarize. As I write this, the Dow Jones Industrial Average stands at 10,544 near the close of trading on Dec. 30th 2009. At the beginning of trading on Oct. 1980, the Dow stood at 932. A gain of 9612 Dow points. If we add all our wining positions and subtract all our losing positions as advocated by this methodology, we have a net gain of 13336 and we have avoided losses of 5710 for a total of 19,046 Dow points. A 98% improvement.

Now, finally, the mystery number will be explained and then the philosophy behind it. If you go to the Bureau of Labor Statistics   web site which is bls.gov, click on payroll employment on the right side of the home page. Click on historical data and it's all right there.

Why does this work so well? Our economy depends on people working! Not on people not working. There are probably hundreds of ways to put a spin on whether the stock market will go up or down. I am not going to even try to refute any one of them. Net monthly payroll change is so basic to our economy that sooner or later those changes affect stock market valuations. If you can miss the effects of major recessions you will do well in the long term.

Some of you may want to see an example of the spreadsheet I have used to write this. I'll include the last year or two and then a blank one with the titles intact so you can do your own recording right in the back of this book. I hope you will put this information to good use and MAKE YOUR MONEY GROW !!

Date	Mystery #	Dow Close	Buy	Sell	4 mo.	3 mo.
1/1/2006	294	10,864			233	278
2/1/2006	274	10,993			277	243
3/1/2006	282	11,109			253	283
4/1/2006	151	11,367			250	236
5/1/2006	24	11,168			183	152
6/1/2006	70	11,150			132	82
7/1/2006	186	11,185			108	93
8/1/2006	149	11,381			107	135
9/1/2006	147	11,679			138	161
10/1/2006	82	12,080			141	126
11/1/2006	261	12,221			160	163
12/1/2006	219	12,463			177	187
1/1/2007	180	12,622			186	220
2/1/2007	36	12,269			174	145
3/1/2007	184	12,354			155	133
4/1/2007	35	13,121			109	85
5/1/2007	156	13,628			103	125
6/1/2007	54	13,422			107	82
7/1/2007	(65)	13,212			45	48
8/1/2007	(28)	13,358			29	(13)
9/1/2007	100	13,896			15	2
10/1/2007	165	13,930			43	79
11/1/2007	215	13,372			113	160
12/1/2007	120	13,265			150	167

Date	Mystery #	Dow Close	Buy	Sell	4 mo.	3 mo.
1/1/2008	(72)	12,443			107	88
2/1/2008	(144)	12,266			30	(32)
3/1/2008	(122)	12,263			(55)	(113)
4/1/2008	(160)	12,820		10,000	(125)	(142)
5/1/2008	(137)	12,638			(141)	(140)
6/1/2008	(161)	11,350			(145)	(153)
7/1/2008	(128)	11,584			(147)	(142)
8/1/2008	(175)	11,544			(150)	(155)
9/1/2008	(321)	10,851			(196)	(208)
10/1/2008	(380)	9,325			(251)	(292)
11/1/2008	(597)	8,829			(368)	(433)
12/1/2008	(681)	8,776			(495)	(553)
1/1/2009	(741)	8,001			(600)	(673)
2/1/2009	(681)	7,063			(675)	(701)
3/1/2009	(652)	7,609			(689)	(691)
4/1/2009	(519)	8,168	5,000		(648)	(617)
5/1/2009	(303)	8,500			(539)	(491)
6/1/2009	(463)	8,557			(484)	(428)
7/1/2009	(304)	9,172			(397)	(357)
8/1/2009	(154)	9,496			(306)	(307)
9/1/2009	(139)	9,712			(265)	(199)
10/1/2009	(127)	9,713			(177)	(135)
11/1/2009	4	10,345			(104)	(87)
12/1/2009	(85)	10,606			(87)	(69)

Date	Mystery #	Dow Close	Buy	Sell	4 mo.	3 mo.
						.